ORDINARY TIME

ORDINARY TIME

Gil McElroy

Talonbooks

Talonbooks
PO 2076, Vancouver, British Columbia, Canada v6b 3s3
www.talonbooks.com

Typeset in ScalaSans & Minion and printed and bound in Canada.

First Printing: 2011

The publisher gratefully acknowledges the financial support of the
Canada Council for the Arts; the Government of Canada through the
Book Publishing Industry Development Program; and the Province of
British Columbia through the British Columbia Arts Council and the
Book Publishing Tax Credit for our publishing activities.

LIBRARY AND ARCHIVES CANADA CATALOGUING IN PUBLICATION

McElroy, Gil
        Ordinary time / Gil McElroy.
Poems.
ISBN 978-0-88922-675-3
        I. Title.
PS8575.E47O74 2011   C811'.54   C2011-902487-X

for Heather

ever & always

Contents

CHAIN HOME

for DHM

No one exactly knows
Exactly how clouds look in the sky
Or the shape of the mountains below them
Or the direction in which fish swim.
No one exactly knows.
The eye is jealous of whatever moves
And the heart
Is too far buried in the sand
To tell.

JACK SPICER

Cobra Judy[1]

Is
of an an, &
aboard. Is
to against. Is
to for, &
quite capable
of.

The wide (or
a wide) available
to aid in. (Can also
perform from.)

Consists
of. Has
a field
of. Is
mounted on a (some, even,
in the).

Controlled,
to ensure
much of, to be
during, required
by, & needed
for – as well
as critical for – use
by all.

The heart,
hung motionless.

Cobra Dane[2]

Is a,
fulfilled & early to others,
of all but
the.

Is an, to
acquire on developing.

Was developed. Was upgraded (including
all of the heart &
its audible past).

Was re-
written, en-
hanced.

Generates approximates,
arranged in, &
radiated through,
together with
designated containings
occupying, roughly,
buildings oriented
toward.

Provided to.

Established by.

Responsible for.

Under a,
by all reasonable to anticipate.

COBRA GEMINI[3]

Transportable (de-
signed to).

Capable of.
Housed for.

Will be,
temporarily. Is,
currently. Was,
eliminated.

Is based (to
provide).

On-targets
are phased,
are transmitted, &
are common.

Width of
& wide-band.

Has a (slaved to),
as well as.

Uses super. Uses double. Uses triple
(respectively).

Runs the
made up of,
which – directed, established,
& validated – used
to use the heart, though
blooded.

Provides processing,
is responsible for, &
will operate
& maintain.
Is one of a,
& funded by.
Is the program
for.

Will validate
& model
& modify, essential
to the use by.

PAVE PAWS[4]

A
triangle,
rapidly. An
elevation, supporting. A
direction, tilted
back.

A
final check
of the heart. The
timing fixed
to another. The
large fix
aimed & entirely
automatic.

The name.

The better beams (commonly aimed & not to blame).

The permissible heart.

White Alice[5]

The white
was scattered. It
was scattered to standards
& line-of-sight.

It
was connected – in some cases
was used.

It
was conceived,
for example, was
installed, was
designed, was
leased, was de-
activated, though
still beating.

Names
were used. (It
was possible.) Each one
was remote. Some
were far. Some
were required. Some
were sometimes connected,
disrupting hearts.

Having
& meaning
both.

TEXAS TOWERS[6]

Off-
shore, &
eastern first

(2, 3, 4).

No
one.

DEW Line[7]

1

Toward zero
dips. The whip
of snow. Talking
across the sky, miles
from any eye to-
ward.

The domes
loomed, were
travelled between. The world
took cover.

2

But say. Said
already, could
speak, cover
an entire continent. Do
with it what-
ever.

3

Effective storms. Man's
land. Radio,
occasionally, threw up much
partially reflected. Sphere
sited, the signal,
& it was at-
mospheric.

4

By
the tundra, by
the buildings, & hard by
the depths by
the tundra.

5

The nature.
The difficulties.

6

Alters. Widens. Latens.

Hearts laid
end to end.

7

The domes came,
planned, manned,
& rechecked. Building
them. Tons
of essential
weeks.

8

Life battles
& isolation
nights. Grace
be good. The health
of the chaplains.

9

Yet
for the
zero

10

Nothing but you
on all sides of me.

LONG LINES[8]

Long
haul, heavy
duty, open
wire

digits

two letters,
so far gone.

Chain Home[9]

In
the early days, warning
couldn't go
out. Early,
for the way might might
strike.

The island, the
height of land, the bits the water
washed. Personnel, they
came, be-
came, moved
on.

Monotony
a popular pastime.

The chain. The units. The remoteness. The factured hearts.

No tracks
plotted.

Yellow Beetle[10]

The reports,
first, were
kept on, you
know.

Then
the navigations (in
secret). The
permafrost (interference un-
predicted). The
differences in determining. Pulse-
matching, no.

Slaves, east
& west. Word
was received – how closing
& for when?

The
predominant tower. The
archaeology.

On the river, years ago.

1,2,3 *are* code names for U.S. military radar systems designed for missile warning and detection, and confirmation of arms control treaties. Cobra Judy is a ship-mounted system, Cobra Dane is located in Alaska, and Cobra Gemini is a transportable system capable of being used on land and sea.

4 *is* a highly sophisticated chain of three United States Air Force radar stations situated in Massachusetts, California, and Alaska charged with the task of missile warning and satellite detection. Unlike typical radar sites, the antennas of PAVE PAWS (PAVE is a military program name; PAWS is an acronym for Phased Array Warning System) do not physically rotate. These stations comprise three-sided pyramidal structures with flattened tops and radar arrays set along each side. The PAVE PAWS site in Massachusetts has been highlighted as a possible cause of elevated rates of certain forms of cancer in nearby populations.

5 *was* a military telecommunication system set up in Alaska by the United States Air Force (USAF) in the 1950s to link air force bases and sites like the Distant Early Warning (DEW) Line to command centres. Rendered obsolete by advances in telecommunications, in the early 1970s it was transferred to civilian use. The last site was in operation until 1985.

6 *were* offshore USAF radar platforms situated in the Atlantic Ocean along the eastern seaboard of the United States. Three platforms – Nos. 2, 3, and 4 – were constructed, and they operated from the late 1950s until the early 1960s. In 1961, a storm destroyed No. 4, taking the lives of its entire crew of twenty-eight. The remaining towers were decommissioned and demolished two years later.

7 *was* a chain of radar sites across the Canadian Arctic and Alaska. Constructed in the 1950s, the DEW Line was designed to keep watch for a Soviet attack from across the North Pole. The advent of the Intercontinental Ballistic Missile (ICBM) rendered it all but obsolete. DHM went up to the Line in 1969 and worked there until it was shut down in the late 1980s.

8 *was* the AT&T network responsible for long distance telecommunications. Established after WWII, it evolved from a system comprising open-wire telephone and telegraph lines to coaxial cable and then microwave communications networks. Its now-obsolete microwave towers can still be found in Canada and the United States. Long Lines introduced direct dialling for long-distance telephone communications in 1951.

9 *was* the code name for a chain of early radar stations established along the coast of England just prior to WWII. Technologically crude by contemporary standards, it was instrumental in the defence of England against German air attacks. A version of Chain Home was set up along the coast of British Columbia and in Atlantic Canada during WWII. DHM spent that war serving in the Royal Canadian Air Force (RCAF), manning remote Chain Home sites located on the Queen Charlotte Islands.

10 *was* a code name used as part of an experimental chain of secret LORAN (LOng RAnge Navigation) stations established in the Canadian arctic in the late 1940s by the RCAF and USAF to provide navigation assistance to military flights in the region. The system (made up of the "master" Yellow Beetle station at the mouth of the Mackenzie River and two "slave" stations to the east and the west) never worked properly and was shut down in early 1950. DHM served at Yellow Beetle from 1949 until its closure. In 1997, the site was archaeologically examined.

Some Julian Days

The lived present holds a past and a future within its thickness.

Maurice Merleau-Ponty

A spot
near the dock,
where the gulls prefer
to gather, I walk
into, herd them
forward

                              reluctance giving way
to wing

In the debris of shells & shit
the beach littered with the remains
of brussels sprouts

                                        2447095

The occasion
fits. Now,   *(Select, she said, & it was done*
where to   *with her hands.)*
install it?

The point
needs the permission   *(The bourgeois love of hands.)*
of instruments.

To forget   *(One thought. Write*
happens.   *it down.)*

24482455

Facts
are habitual. Like
a knowledge of bark or
secret cartels.

The some-
times-fact of light –
being so light,
weightless like
light – settles into
the voids between
astronomy, forbidden & unworkable words
in the air.

Ineradicable speech.

The reminded flight
of birds.

2448256

A rather
odd mist up here. Or
I could simply be
out of landscape.

Shadows pass
in the bright space behind
things.

The geographical
happens, my shoes proof
of ground.

2448263

From
every living
thing so-called
anecdotes, fictions
& memory. My
hunger began
in tense, in
the terrible winds
of that city.

But
enough now
to swim upon. Are
these drums
really intended?
I can feel
a reorientation of the light
& even the cumulative effects
of the atmosphere.
But the slightness
of the tide
escapes the aware part
of my brain.

The east
appears, anonymous.
& a lot of cedars. I look at snowflakes
& undertake the commitment
of gifts.

To crawl should come
next.

2448342

Something, to
me, not intended. It has
nothing to do with
description. It's
not to happen, it's
too far to carry around.

The judgements
for which I would wake
possess wishes, & the wishes & residues
of the preceding thing.

One underestimates
the place.

The piano simile impinges upon life.

What's the use of a whole run of instances?

The nearest sky is much more numerous.

2449326

Depth is constant,
landscape mythical.
The whole damned idea finds it
all motives,
& offhand.

This is my language now.

I'm looking at it.

Right now.

It is a fabric
among all possible.

2449354

Was life,
& so forth.
'Course,
we can now pose
& stump the heart with rules,
acts of deed which aggravate,
& the living themselves.

I am often
from the heart, die-
hard, even,
but once again
simply cold.

2452490

If you were,
you might. Lived,
there would be
no recipe,
& could contain atoms
at all.

I can't solve
a single molecule. Two
dimension, four
dimensions, the strong,
strong force – things (& indeed
the odious gases
in the normal
world) would be
obeyed.

2452494

The in-
terrupted process
of a tear, implicit but also
closed.

Fields like
their eyes
half-closed with the necessity
of æther.

Dormant lashes. Cheeks
beneath.

2452541

Outbreaks
of a German
mood on either side
of the hand.

By
today's large standards & voltages,
manipulations are un-
deniable.

The weight
of long, poignant handwritings bruises
the false,
yet mutual,
hand.

But, &
mostly other,
they do.

2452548

Mauves, I
thought, the
fresh fruit
of sequence.

Yet
we move,
no name
for it, to
a dark
beyond tasting.

2452560

The daily cycle
of the dead
would think
& be cause,
hunted so
by parts.

Emulation
is furtive,
the depths
an instance.

Genesis,
then, a magic
we can see as eyes & a brow are
distantly fashioned.

2452768

Alone
& light

everything
suitably re-
buffed

No
amount of
outlines clarify
this world

What they are you are
in the lie of slope
& numbness of
howevers

2453078

Missed
our first grandson's birth
                    wasn't there
that November day

though 12 later
he slept on my stomach,
woodstove burning bright, cold
Cape Breton wind
shaking the house

Made it
for our second's

family taking turns holding him for pictures

came my turn
I sang to him
the only song
whose words
I know
                    Bruce Springsteen
                    "Thunder Road"

O, come take my hand …

& jeez
he did

                              2453199
                              for Keegan & Logan

We are to
one another, one
entangled choice close
outside the body/We

are
something
that still even the eventual depends upon moments
after touch, the
mere fact
warm/Welcome

The words, the
fortune, the
very mood
of heaven

2453416
for Heather

The day framed
by Sun,
by Moon

one behind, one
before

driving west
between approximate
things

toward
the setting
one

2453811

The sweet is
outgrown (& in any event
sprinkled with
the logic
of things), so
there's no sweet to the sherry, nor
to the syllables of it

but in front
of bridges, I shall work
a great delight.

2453904

Today requires
a past

The riverside road
closed, silent
& utterly still for the first time
in who knows
how long

          The house
slowly pulled
from origin A
to destination B, stopping for the night
at the exact point between us
& the river

A new view – all gables
& dormers – inserted into
the old, the river
displaced

            this strategy
assembled here, this action
having weight
& many bits
of order

       this
stuff of periods

                        2453933

West
    (again)

Orion over
my left shoulder, the
Hunter, a
Giant
      rising

Betelgeuse his
shoulder

the red giant

rising

                        2453976

Twice
from love she sat
through death

friend (first),
& mother (years
later)

      father, al-
most

that
November night
shared

Hard times/wordless stances
in the world of change

           2454100

The dictum
of comets

The Moon,
too

& the one
magnetic field

2454167

In our
us form all things
named

mythic us,
reasoned ago & reached yet darkening the tests, the
anatomists of
them

everything about the tickle
thick with addition

2454496

Map right to
map left – the
machine perspective ('62
Chevy, new
then)

Between the window
& my father's
shirts, back seat me
on the left – sisters (two,
then) middle
& right

Crossing
the continent water
to water – all
the unremembered data
of the act
save

for the small death of leaving, the
snow (Grand Forks), the
Easter arriving,
then

                              2454961

ORDINARY TIME
(9 Propers)

Ordinary Time comprises the two periods – one following Epiphany, the other following Pentecost – which do not fall under the "strong seasons" of Advent, Christmas, Lent, or Easter.

WIKIPEDIA

Proper 1

S

Console the cry. Seemly periods
double, guilt
voices away.

The grass withers
with the breath of it, but the words – well, here
are their arms, their
rewards, gathered
& held.

Here
is the press of all things, & now,
now as far from again. You loved
with the oil of rivals,
& the heavens – well, they
passed by.

In the world, this
world, the word was not
one thing, was not
light &/or darkness (it
a man to bear).

M

The sea
in hand, the nearest
inch, nearest
bushel …

See the buckets?
See the coasts & islands? The
counting & emptiness? Some-
one – *someone* – chose.

Did you/had
you/was it not
you, you who

sat & stretched out,
withered, & was
carried away?

Having once
heard & never
failed, with
the dead in hand, with
the age underfoot fulfilled
& close at hand
making you at once
go & leave
because there was a man & he, so astonished,
shouted behind it …

T

Let us assemble
coasts & islands. Fasten them
with nails to keep them
steady.

I grasped you.
I told you, "Crimes made up your living,"
& the air rebelled, we too
amongst it. The rest of the world,
well, how extra-
ordinary that no-
one could claim
credit.

Feverish hands
helped & brought those
who were because
they knew a lonely place & its
companions. This neighbourhood proclaimed because
our knees stretched once, but then
again no longer.

First Quarter. Algol, demon
star, dims. Places
keep coming.

W

The water & its tongue
shall open
onto dry ground – planes
& boxes side by side
as though
the hand produced
what was going
to happen. Revealed
& known, at least, done
less to than mud.

I send you, if
asked, altogether nothingness
& wind.

The roof. The stretcher. Now,
some talk these thoughts.

Easier to get up, pick
up, go
off.

Like this.

T

Here
is my light. It does not
break or snuff. It
will not
grow faint.

Who hammered? What
came of it? I made the light. See how things
are before I tell you everything
left in it, even, thinking
in front of the door
of the roof they'd made an opening
in.

F

I have called,
& by rivers walked. I have given, in return, north
& south, & back from
far away. Which of them
brings me back?

This name grows
firm.

S

[…]

Proper 2

S

For your sake I
shall make a way, a
path. Look: I
am making a road & bestowing
rivers.

But, no. No need
to remember, to
think. I am done doing.
You have,
&, having,
your weariness is sur-
named, un-
alterable, heir to a tenth of the names
given. Hurry, eat! Look around,
already!

M

I am there, these things
dispelled & to me redeemed. Who went
down? Who went
up? Was it
something tossed hither & thither? Gusts,
maybe, or tricks
of delicious deception all just a part
of the work? I'm boat-
ready, afflicted in any way
forward, summoned
& sent. Drive
on.

T

The makers
& the works pose
the nothing that shame
casts. The charcoal, the
hammer, the
chalk outline making it look
like a house – a
house among trees planted
& nourished, the Moon
full. Here, take
part of it. This half
is replete.

We know
nothing, stand
by nothing. Over the embers, something
in my hand is right
& wrong. From now on
more lies.

Such a crowd
collects at a meal. Mother
& brother ask
for you.

W

Thus spread I, I
who foiled & made foolish, who
confounded & confirmed,
& made the plans
succeed. Who say
I shall? Who say
to the ocean, saying
"level"
          "shatter"
                    "smash"?
In your lot, once,

the coarse effects
of such goodness wanted
of you. Showed you
up, even.

Once again
lakeside, the whole crowd
gathered round. Seed
fell. Birds
came. Thorns
grew.

T

I am here, though
armed. Rain
& clouds let with,
given orders
about the heavens
& their array.

So lives like
senseless people with wine
saved the whole thing. Water
would've been glorious, wrinkled
& faultless.

But one of you
loves himself (sic). He brought in
the bed, the lampstand kept hidden, kept
secret. He also said
what you are hearing.
He also said
which is the smallest (& used
many words).

F

For he is
who set it
firm, I have not spoken. I did not say. There is

no saving me. By mine
own self be. What comes
comes in shame. Uprightness
demands it. Mother may
I? Heartedly

             willingly

                              &

                                        without threats.

S

The burden, the
loads no one can save
until old age, until
your hair is grey – I myself shall carry, lavish
& weighted. Lift
it up. Put
it down,
so that never
replies, never
says the things that happened
long ago.

I said
I shall do
what I have
said.

Your
belt. Your
feet of faith.
& your helmet. Speak
fearlessly, so that you know
precisely, imperishably. In all,
the burning will make itself
known.

You reached
the lake because you
had the strength, though
many were
earnest. In the country
people came, dressed,
were afraid, as you were the man
begged to be
allowed.

All done.

Proper 3

S

Step
on the ground. Remove your tie. Loll about
& think, in spite of yourself.
Take the meal,
& listen.

Your wishes delude you.

We have, let's
say, flesh filled with,
& yet free from, science
& pure water. Hope
made us, hope
we professed – not
absence, as some
say, but each other,
& again.

Eight years
lying there. They asked you
to walk around.

Things like this.

M

Listen to your
name. I knew your neck,
& your genteel forehead,
too, though
your ears not. As I told you before,
you did it. Why won't
you admit it? Until today
I've been patient, my mouth
obstinate. But you heard
nothing.

From & by,
human being human, me
dead to peace …

Wicked!

I am who was called, not
that there was trouble.
You were there – was anyone else convinced?
Was I trying
not to be preached at? Being
that I taught it, it
was surely heard. In my
limitless traditions, who had time when
I was in a hurry?

Seeing you
earnestly sick, your hands
pressed one under another – the touch
at once dried up, aware of
clothes. You see,
all around.

T

Listen,
the heavens assembled. Which of them
loved you? If only you numbered
their names.
Come near,
& say, "Go." Make
water. Split
rocks.

After that
it will be gone again, quite sure
& fruitless – one moment
preached & to you promised, recognized
or not.

The contrary
edged me, leaving
home. This wisdom,
surely, there & amazed. Twelve pairs
or nothing. Wore
a spare. Wore
sandals until
you refused to shake them off.

W

Last Quarter (coasts,
pay attention). My
birth made my name, hid
me, made me concealed. But
I have exhausted
all the whiles,
& now my eyes shall make & see,
keeping apart
from insincerity. You gentile, you – you compel someone?
Follow that sin! Build some-
thing!

We
used to have heard this. Now
it was the same to have
& do so, leading
oaths.

The girl. The
mother. The
head.

T

Mountains feel
no pity. I have palms, so
go away. Your eyes, you – will you put them on me
once more? This place
is too cramped. I am beckoning & hoisting, you
stupid man. Is only
one me.

Him, he said – him
for a while. Could be
he saw them going. He saw them
without & lonely, the Moon
far.

F

Where is yours
by which I repudiate?
Is my hand covered?
I have offered my cheeks
& know that I am moth-eaten. This
is what you will
lie down upon. To put it once: once
ratified, hundreds abolish it. You see
promise, but I
see progeny making
no exception.

The wind
came & all at once,
hard pressed
through & through.

S

Consider
the quarry. Consider
when I called.
But pity will turn my arm. About the coasts & islands:
there can be neither. There can be
neither for you. Eat
without washing. You
say things for the sake
of other things,
& someone uncleans something. Understand? It goes
into the stomach & the heart. Things
come undone.

Proper 4

S

My awake arm was not
pierced, was not
ransomed. You forget who spreads out
the earth. You never stopped
that day, when I was bent
& trembling.

I was stirred up. My name
was in your mouth, my hand
awake.

It is by. It was because. It was because now it is. It was through.

All these.

My, but
it comes. But
anyone will,
whether when someone seeks
or not.

Why do you
crow? You work at it. You
circumcise someone broken, yet you want to say
you know me because no one
but *no one*
laid a hand on me.

M

He said, "Your feet, they start on a journey," but he, he went home.
Look, he did nothing, now, but came here, dazed. Anyone else
here?

The sun rose. Next morning, the place was plain.

Forget the living. The ages, the world – it was so, and for that, was
upright. It was because, and now was without. It was when

someone took care. It was the call, the knowing, but not because (*not* because). It was not bread. It is not *my* bread, it is *the* bread, & gives way. I am no one, no one you can see because I have not to do, now. It is this & that.

T

Eight days
grown & watched. Weaned,
even, not to share a skin of wine
& some bread – all/any of these things
promised & welcomed unless
drawn from me.

W

It happens. Offer him
one of the mountains, then
chop wood & start
the fourth day. Then
look, take
the knife, & swear
that you have not
loved.

Tell me
the subject & the way of a promise. Promise,
now! Discuss the tests. Bread
them in the boat. Do
you not see, not
remember? I
broke thousands.

T

The length
of a hundred years I can
remove, low
to the lunation
& demure constants. Let

me have the field. I
will make it
good enough, & I
shall bury its boundaries. I
shall refuse release, be pilloried, sawn, or stoned, be
in want of treats, even, with clouds
thrown in, the Sun eclipsed. You should,
you know, see this: the ring (annular), the
words, the
outset away …

This was
who was.

F

By man
his thighs
to choose.

Should I
draw water
& drink?

I have
a pitcher.

Thought such,
yet had
grief.

Near this
place, known
acts done.

S

Tell me
what you'd
had heard.
Provide straw,
eels, &

water. Take
this property
to him –
now. *Now.*

Your crooked
limbs made
trouble. What
you knew
afterwards you
had gathered
whole. Speak.
Refuse. Escape.
Voice that
thing, &
therefore please.
Anyone will
know. But
when crowds
want judgement,
they want
the pears
no one
has.

Proper 7

S

From,
or no, you
came, next morning saying,
"Let so."

Master up
the proper names of wrangling. Who keep
the straight path? Who have
all gone claiming? Not all
are made of wood.

For all this
I am yet indigent. Let the little
not stop. A man
ran up this question: "Must I do?"
& I said,
"More."

M

This
is the story: how
[it] was barren. Why go on
living? Bread
up.

We were
those, some
& some. Such
rabble, descended
from.

T

Famine,
for present, shall
be with you, shall

give all, shall
make you.

Place
will kill you,
the windows
of account. You
should have
incurred. Try.
Fold. Become
rich.

Watch, the Moon
full, because you must. Not
a grief, mind. I
envy you words. Why, in time
you to all (they all went
home, & at daybreak
alone standing
there) you
got to say, "Let the one
be the first!" then
writ them,
apt.

Heard this?

W

Good, anyone,
that there
he saw
& wondered.

So he
wrapped his
head, put
on like
a tunic,
& to the west
he feared.

Through
the given,
the same
of us, you must be
another come
to others.

I am
anyone,
but will.

T/F

As soon as
blessings were seized, [he] said, "Who
brought me?" Cried out
& took, hearing loudly
a name.

Blessings
I have, but will
shake for
my words.

Any pre-
tence to an-
other comes to
others, half-
heartedly. Bless
them in sorrow standing. Touch
coals.

They
[come] from you – in all,
everyone but
so. What is
what I speak? Is what
you learn? A man as I have
is not doing. I
did not, but
it was never
spoken.

Prefer
in speaking.

S

A well
& water.

Tears.

Flesh, shapely
fallen.

Give in to argument. Who
does it? Whether
fall he shall, or
others equal, who
knows. Dent
the one from eating, & make
none of us
die. Why himself does
another brother? God then gives
an account, that none
can bring someone within from what
springs which.

Proper 8

S

So few
days to go, took
& came.

I may be able,
in case, to
know of the living, the
truth. Mystery,
indeed!

I am justified/seen/ pro-
claimed/believed in/taken up – have
really digested, have
always been so,
demure.

It holds,
& now
a saying: a
camel, a
needle.

Me

you

or the land.

M

This made
& retorted:
so birth too
shall have him.

Who
is this? Whose clothes
have I?

I trod,
I trampled.
I looked,
even.

I was appalled/crushed/shattered.

One day,
one harvest.

Something which
we have, which
we have & touch – *this*
is that life. We
saw it (the demon star dimmed), declared
what was & what had been. We are
what we have seen. We must
carry the night.

Having ground, who
has been washed?
Call my eyes
off.

They asked.
So I answered.

T

Were
at our, saw
was not,
& I, where towards my past, have
worked. Me,
& yet claimed,
given it on me. Were that
the dream – a piebald
thing – made
vows outwitted.

Not the
only outcome,

you know. It has
children. You
a new one? Watch,
be lost,
& 'ward it (the
teaching of it).

You trust it
in person, asking of yours,
"So?"

How
plied.

W

I have
let by. I have
let go to each day. Look: where
are the mercies? O,
that they would open, as fire makes
the air all unexpected. No ear
for our sake, keeping
us upright (we, the clay, yes, all
of us).

I am
because – because I have & you do not.
The world is passing.

In all,
who herds? One
them out, each those that my voice
failed.

In all I am,
the good/the hired/the abandoned

I know I lie,
but must.

T

I shall
the country, one
they will not foul, them,
though low
& practised.

The lived ever gone, but
from this hour. They had,
but they never
if they had. But not,
not because & because. Hear
in the treetops sparrows falling, the Moon full. The head need be
afraid.

F

I & all, when I strike, know
the day. Too
will know.

So now
take pity – grace
& all. When I gather tries, they
will know, face out. They must
by letting. The reason
is that it did, my dear, but what we are
we shall be because
we is.

Now you are
well appeared. Away!
Whoever lives to undo, whoever does
& does not, is not. Say what you are
when. Forward them. Have
gone.

S

The trance of streams
flows east. Water
leads me, flowing out
& leading across my ankles. Sand
& stream. Knees.
Waist, now.
Deep.

When I name
rivers, the water
teems, the banks
never fail. The marshes
will not,
no.

This
is the which
that we must not, do
not, if the world
cause this. Our love is
but something.

Do not
bring. I
have. Cross
& worry.

Cold water
causes.

Proper 9

S

She raises squares.
She calls out.
She delivers you.

How much attention when
your whirlwind downed, when you
had not, spurned
& choked, but would
& always? Give us those not
inner. Gone, all
to themselves.

So it is.

Know what
drink shall be
at your right
hand, mine
to which became not
first & ransomed.

M

My, for
as those discovered, those
who gain yield beyond
nothing. In their
right, in their
left, ways are filled, paths
are lead, heaven is
cleft open.

Mere talk,
brother, bound up
with cloth.

T

Listen! Pay
attention! What I am
do not forsake!

The bread, the
wine, the
path.

This
is what keeping overcomes, & this
is not without,
but with water. So
there!

Many visit among a town
bordering there.

W

If you have
words

if you have
committed your
lips

do this.

Go.

No one
gives, yet all
gather a little, a little
folded in.

Let us
love, since love
fails. This
is that that we might
consist in – this, this
but dear, & whoever sees
sees.

Is what
I speak.

T

Keep. Bind these.
Write them
down.

Say.

Call.

Under-
stand.

While I was
I saw. I
noticed, going along at twilight,
& looked, seeing
my feet.

I
lurked. I
caught (I
had to – this
is why I
came).

I
spread. I
sprinkled.
Come on, forthwith, until
we wheedle
& know
whatever we
know. I am not saying
we are well. We
are as we are, true
& this, near the one come, near
the dead.

The feet.

The hair.

The ointment.

The money
said this, said,
"Leave the day. Have
me."

F

Is not?
Is not the voice? I
am my words. Listen
when I speak. My
mouth [is] up-
right, everything
[is] straight.

Count my hands.

Meanwhile,
the next day
was what
called.

(Another
sign.)

S

Before
(from the
very beginning), before
the hills. Before
the first elements
fixed, thickened, assigned,
traced, I was at play, through dance again
possessing hands, among at,
these from.

Now what shall I say?

PROPER 10

S

To be made, all
blood & abundance,
mercy given us
through

                    this, *this*
is time perish-
able – short sorts
of uptight ordinals.

Low me. The camel. The needle. The
astonished eye.

M

No years.
Words of stone.
Lives that slip.

Take yourself
from your heart, full
of appeal. Have you reckoned the notion
of edges? We do. We do – selves
of certain measure
creased (& not with assurance) in
to many words:

our	*may*	*you*	*your*	*on*	
give	*&*	*as*	*in*	*&*	*but*

Yes, you
yours.

The using.

T

Hence, that
you this, as

what you own, to
tire, to
crawl in the shade. Heart
since. The
knot of any
image.

Now,
who is humble? I wish you
little volition, be it
ever so boastful, or
vexing to the end. But consider
that there is someone speaking – some-
one else. Careful,
you! Wash
your face.

The lamp follows.

W

With a mouth,
better. Filled with
talk, no one
laughs. Fine
           & foolish
                   & false

Who
brings it? Come on, who
absolves?

Before the dead, avaricious children.

Wander a place. I
come from, go
off, go
in, tidy towards, constant
& most.

T

No
is worth
the day. Yes
makes it. Shoulder
both. Pay
the fear of
the path of
will not
go, no.

Dead messages.

                "Do
instruct people, but their ears will be
new & their own."

The time
of myths, ill
in turn. Look, I
told: "Am going," & "not
come!"

Having you,
I dip the granting
hand.

F

Customs: learn
them from
the heart between you, any above
& any under. Must
not misuse, male
& female. (Must not. Must not. Must
not.)

Were
the words there
when you
bled?

A fool that those
at all. A true you. I
am more than I have, more,
than then, then by
trickery.

The narrow & the hard.
Sheep. Wolves. Fruits. Thorns.

Day comes.
& so
many miracles.

S

Heard this,
you: seen that, should
we again?

The right to left way. Be
once, but next time be
not (if
only). Grow
perfect. Have
one another.

These points.

The besieged message.

PROPER 11

S

In consequence
In use
In having
In becoming
In decision
In according
In notwithstanding
In adequate
In translation

Goes
Stands
Sets
Turns
Stills
Remains

Go along down.
Set off.
Go up & join.
Run.
Sit.
Refer.

M

I thought,
"Try," & this
was futile, this
hand, this
pleasure. So made
my eyes it all
was, away
from you, over
to seek heaven or
God's curse. Now you,
& the sure, the
field, the

setting down. (Yes,
the setting down.)

T

The wind, the
Sun – under
both &
full of. We
were, but those, those
we saw, recognized
their right hands, their
country, their
own houses.

W

A time,
etc.

T

& I
thought, thinking
to myself breath-
ing, of
the one
& both, of
the practices in
messages lavishly sent, reckoning,
then, on the books of practice (to put it
even once).

The crowds
heard of this, but
we had with us
fish enough.

F

[...]

S

But what
all? No one
joying under
the sun.

Apart from
sweet, a son
nothing to his
mother.

The passing heart.

IMAGINARY TIME

One can think of ordinary, real, time as a horizontal line. On the left, one has the past, and on the right, the future. But there's another kind of time in the vertical direction. This is called imaginary time, because it is not the kind of time we normally experience. But in a sense, it is just as real, as what we call real time.

STEPHEN HAWKING

Sometimes a word will start it, like
Hands and feet, sun and gloves.

JOHN ASHBERY

(THE CONQUEST) OF BREAD
after Kropotkin

1

(One)

& yet
ideal.

Later on,
groups (to
a great extent).

In
maintaining centuries, we
learned, by
distance grew rich. The median came, in
this direction chaperoning the leading ideas
of a hand once seized by rubbery & scoured
sampling some
of the bygone implements.

Ah,
the bygones, the
spoils. During since years, treasures
pierced the forest: an
acre of implements & effete old rulers prudently at ease – fifty
or sixty families' worth (the
terrible years of Napoleon
now the stuff
of periods).

Incoming.
& other. The
very high. The
low.

Let me, then, correct
the paint of things; I've no compunction about
someone else's palate, and have
granaries to satisfy.

Truly
we are native
to a humiliating
course. Truly
the old, shopworn dramas
lingered in mindsets that skulls
split. The confession – the
apparent confession – was no defence against
tomorrows, only another way
toward redundancy. I remember
one drawing – a
proper pose, a
subject found upright as if looking to transcend
gravity – & the violent source
of its existence.

Different ways
of totality. Truly white regions of bread appeared
at the centre of stretches, not at
the awkward, toured
edges, eye-
high corners, or
crusty 19th century
horizons.

Lo,
the prodigies. The
nearly completed
overhand left behind
smaller circles & mostly measured
yeasts. This,
then, is our
cheat.

2

Nor do we want
Rothschilds. Their
terrible lisped
quantities sharpened two hundreds of lifetimes
to excess.

3

Bang into
Helium, heart-
ened. See in it
teeth. Be
characterized by large dogs
& societies of
cunning. Range
on.

What else
or not? Much,
much harder forces
of nature, the
three standard clouds (*cirrus, cumulus, stratus*)
& very precise
rising bodies do be-
low.

Big wires & blueprints.

The barbed afflictions of the hand.

Kinds of coins.

Those things,
prating.

4

Small,
& a person's hands, the
one & perhaps posture, nothing
walled in
by destiny. To
build up
hunches. To
complain of salt – feckless spreads within,
& when. Art,
but without rec-
tangles.

5

Half-
decades, laxly. Clearly
the result of the Sun
& some
perpetually basic goddesses linked up
with acceleration. Once
there was a way built
to Newton's stars
& five kinds
of anything, fine
as given. But after France the world moved
by *any* motion,
& strict
British
production.

Things, satisfactorily,
sum to zero. In a few,
laws. Noxious thinks (suffice it
& so). The immense bakeries
we have sought
were evident
to all.

6

We
lost our will
to build a world
in place of the Sun, wrath
penetrating flesh & rigid bones. The
six truths of time, never-
theless, the
rich, who fought
their pastimes, burning off
such un-
workable facts with tidy
English profits.

Warms welcome
the good fortune. This
was, would be, for
along. Religion, sure, but
with results.

7

Tight, hard-
rimmed teeth, the
mass of ex-
foliations, reactions
to green – recent things
to be shed seven times seven. Eye-
high corners. Congenial
steel. The
Moon, too.

Different ways
of totality, there
was. This
fascinating spectacle of shoes,
& all sorts of growing: it
was basic to the eye – per-
petually basic. Minute, even. My
things matched.

On one slope
was a door, clearly amiable. A way
was built to its closing, a
successful metric
way

8

8th century
tyrants.

9

In the in-
correct, the
mathematics of time
was assumed, the
possibility that today
we might matter behind
the enabled things was
unposed.

Ah, the bonuses
of oxygen. The
fully operational years assumed
stances designed for their
thin plastic days
& balsawood nights. God
was had by theft. The weather
stood by. The world
became a white-
out, no?

Nein. The
cooling & meandering were mere
acts of half-dimensions, dirt-finessed
& cajoled, so to leaven the Sun
on the longest of days.

10

At
every meal, she
told me
something – in
sorrow begging, in
secret fasting. I
dipped, actually, at all her
pretty good answers in my head. Adversity
& affliction was
a broth without
any.

Eating fetched us
half-worths. Whoever had
a longer table
won.

But
I took a loaf
& looked on, the
antonyms & lunchbox voices all around me quarrelling royally
with some that shalt eat
the white stuff.

URBAN CREATURES

The iron in
the chapter – ships
or not – begins
with rigid tramlines (*symbolic*
tramlines).

These are
two sorts of amples (the very
birds of culture)
& a hankering for
the comparable.

The nouns should
be secondary.
The teeth & turf should
not glitter with filial focus. I
should not preach
today.

As Lightning

In
the beginning, my
front legs so much
as string
& mister-knit
stories.

The points became
rifles, such a posture
that was tactical – nothing walled-
in by destiny – that
the network of rememberings became
a thing in the veins.

& so here
we are, practising
latitudes.

ONE-HUNDRED-DOLLAR MATTERS

We stand
sure, those who
earned of ourselves the Moon now silent, there to stand
& not to add to the unspeakable extreme
in distance

a line
of manipulative doors in
the neatness of the disappearing, in
the expunging of
sunny spots
& stains beautiful, if difficult, streaming all the orange
away

Eventual Days

What autumn,
to the daggers
of Europe. On
what slope
is the suppression of steppes, on
what other
them extreme atomists?

Things match. Calendars
continue.

Jack Elliott

Good will.

Be sure
of it, for here we have
a planet where insomnia increases
at night, & latent men of straw
impinge upon
music – music
appearing like elation thinking over
the very meagre names
of night.

Devilish things
we are, surrounded
by older & more local
times shaped
like pine cones

or
chairs set well back
from the pity to offset
all the soliloquies.

MANY BITS OF ORDER

The best
chemical world presented us
almost pastoral boots. Leave
them in this dirt, its
dark stars
of particles sinister
& inimitable.

Maybe
the yellowcake
would have been
appropriate, as much of it action
as weight.

The half-
life, forever.

ABSTRACT INFECTIONS

Now,
suppose the fine approach
fails, the
colour coupled, the
flavour not. Boggling,
I know.

No point
in consorting about
this. Mess
with the fixes. Think
of the textbooks. Don't
let the pretty bad emergencies
know you.

ATTEMPTED HANDBOOKS

Rather than
a practical story, or
a series of second-in-command
painters, in-
stead

a camouflaged piece of sundown

the optical properties of significance

well-hidden weather

the genre of years

gloves sort of organized

Bath (Again)

Of course
it's Europe!
& this, this
is 1955, everybody
shouting, wanting to mess
with the fixes …

We
were all going to be
engaged in tries, & spent days absorbed
in in-
fatuations.

Never had
such heroisms
failed!

Detours through Mistrust

What of
the rash, poised
to be visible, the
standard hours, the
questions unfamiliar to
wonder – never,
though, the noises
of unthought
vices.

What is perceived keeps
too far
off.

SURE POINTS & LUBRICANTS
for rob m.

Irony, be
a giant. Offer me
no more
of the mill. I'll
overlook the
drawer – so
mellow &
straight – &
the gaudy childhood,
too.

I'll
sing (from right
to left) the wit
of impossible
songs, mimicking the style
of Mancini himself (at the
core), or maybe
Bacharach
beyond high school. Ah, those
were handsome times,
of sure points
& lubricants.

Much gasps.

To pall,
likely.

ELECTROMAGNETIC BEASTS

Our view
is like
this: at first glance
small, third place
in nature,
even.

This is
my best example
of magnets. Hold
your acceptable hands
applied to it – not
like they say but
just so, to remind me
of other electromagnetic
words.

The palms of your hand.

The colour.

The flavour.

No, not
the flavour – the
reassuringly grey briefcases we jiggle
over great distances.

FLUIDLY, SURE

A thing
like a
metre – a
thing not often unhampered – & the Sun (this, too, in
evidence), bang
right into the dog-like
granite.

I'm
troubled by schisms, the leavings
of up & down. My customs
are one-handed. These here fingers
are long in confidence, drawn out
like summer, & may lead
to a collection
of species.

Mother called,
some things
ago.

EVEN TODAY

Even today
we're comparing
shortest points
(our own,
& by us) with the curvature
of ambition,
lascivious
as the family
goes.

It has
to be
wanted. It had
been
an affair,
this is
to say, of
images predicting
a footy ground, useful,
yet.

Sharpless 140

I measure
two seconds, but
much
more
slowly.
The main bits, with
actual chunks, here go on madly,
just as highly
up with stars beyond
story.

Triangles
are equally
subtle, favoured with
the same
radical
& often messy
squinting.

So hitch.

THE Y TRUTH

The grasp
of mechanics, the
leavings
of up & down
celebrating some
point, nipple-
coloured
& with hardly *any*
indignation.

The lean
& hungry sexes, the
ravishing coat, the
migraines, the
mosquitoes

& un-
reconstructed me,
fluidly sure, all
water & white virtuosity.

The Genius of Necessary Parts

It's
not a matter
of cliffs, or
the full 'scape
of lime.

It's
grasped
(& was), rakish,
because a month of safekeeping,
& an instance altogether random,
had a corollary going (all
select arms & eyes, even,
the cuttlefish example wrongly isolable
on the basis of an ingenuous earth,
the group containing humans, select
hairs & eyes, & a few years of
one cloud), that
after a time of hats
& hard, reactionary days, death
could cause such a thing

or organize
any number of acorns of importance
thru the early enigmas of summer
rising un-
abashed.

A Summary of Dinosaurs

The exceptional
atmosphere, after
tents, takes on the form
of several
metres.

Bars
break.

Chain Home was published on-line in *17 seconds: a journal of poetry and poetics* 1 (Fall 2008), & also as a privately printed chapbook.

Julian Day 2454100 and *Julian Day 2453933* appeared on-line in blueskiespoetry.ca on September 14 & 17, 2009, respectively.

Julian Days 2453933, 2453078, 2452560, 2452548, 2452541, and *2448256* appeared in *Sunfish* (U.K.) 1 (Winter 2009).

Ordinary Time (The Propers 1 – 4) was published on-line in *experiment-o* 2 (November 2009).

Ordinary Time (The Propers 7 – 11) appeared in *Dusie* (Switzerland) 9, vol. 3, no. 2 (June 20, 2010).

(The Conquest) of Bread appeared in *Sunfish* (U.K.) 3 (Winter 2010).

Many Bits of Order was published on-line by Angel House Press on April 5, 2009, as part of National Poetry Month.

Bath (Again); Detours Through Mistrust; Electromagnetic Beasts; Fluidly, Sure; Even Today; Sharpless 140; & The Genius of Necessary Parts appeared in *Sunfish* (U.K.) 2 (Summer 2010).

Sure Points & Lubricants was published as above/ground broadside #248.

My deepest thanks to Karl & Christy Siegler, rob mclennan, Amanda Earl, & Nigel Wood.

Thanks also to the Canada Council for the Arts for financial assistance during the writing of some of these poems.